Train Wreck!

by Edie Kast

PEARSON

Scott
Foresman

Editorial Offices: Glenview, Illinois • Parsippany, New Jersey • New York, New York
Sales Offices: Needham, Massachusetts • Duluth, Georgia • Glenview, Illinois
Coppell, Texas • Ontario, California • Mesa, Arizona

In 1820, the United States had been an independent nation for a little more than forty years. Back then, daily life was different from what it is now. Most Americans lived in rural areas. There was no electricity. There were no phones. This was a time before airplanes or automobiles.

Texas, Oregon, and California didn't belong to the United States yet. Native Americans hunting and living on their ancestral lands still controlled vast areas of the West. This was the **era** when railroads were developed, which soon changed the face of our nation.

The Railroad Era Begins

In 1830, there were only twenty-three miles of railroad tracks in the whole United States. By 1930, there were more than 400,000 miles of rails! To lay those tracks, and to build safe trains to ride them, took a lot of hard work. It also took the lives of many workers and passengers.

The very first "railroads" were called "wagonways." These wagonways were roads along which wooden rails were set. The wheels of carts and wagons could roll more smoothly over these rails than they did over rutted dirt roads. Such wagonways were in use in Germany more than four hundred years ago.

By the late 1800s, iron rails had replaced the wooden ones, and special wheels with grooves to

keep the wheel on the track were developed. Then in 1804, the first steam-powered locomotive came on the scene. This engine hauled a five-car train filled with ten tons of iron and seventy men over nine miles of countryside in Wales.

By 1825, both passengers and freight were traveling on the Stockton and Darlington Railroad Company's railway in England. This was the first company to offer regularly scheduled train service. By 1830, such train service was available in the United States.

You'd imagine that everyone would want to ride the new trains. That wasn't true. Some people thought trains were a bad idea. Most people, however, were very excited about this new way of getting from place to place!

Go West!

By 1840, there were already more than 2,800 miles of railway stretching across nine states. Naturally, early trains were different from today's trains. At one time, you risked death to ride a train! It took the effort of many inventors to design trains that worked safely.

As Texas, Oregon, and California became states, Americans began dreaming of a transcontinental railroad. They were thrilled at the idea of a railroad that stretched from coast to coast.

In 1863, work began on the transcontinental railroad. The Central Pacific Railroad company started laying track in Sacramento, California, building east, and the Union Pacific Railroad company started in Omaha, Nebraska, building west.

Railroad workers had to lay more than 1,700 miles of new track. Builders blasted through mountains, crossed plains, and bridged rivers.

Most of the workers on the Central Pacific line were Chinese immigrants. The railroad company even advertised in China for more workers to come to the United States, for they needed lots of men. In 1868, more than 12,000 Chinese men were working on the Central Pacific line.

Unfortunately, Chinese workers were not treated fairly. They were paid only $30 a month, while other workers received $35 a month and room and board.

At first it was hard to get enough people to work on the Union Pacific line. Once the Civil War was over, though, many veterans of that war came to work on the railroad. Irish immigrants were also a large part of the Union Pacific workforce. When work got started in earnest, the Union Pacific laid an average of two miles of track each day.

Race to the Finish

Tunneling through the Sierra Nevada in California was difficult and dangerous work. It involved many difficult steps.

First, workers lowered a man on ropes down the mountain, where he drilled holes in the cliff. He put explosives into those holes and lit the explosives. When he jerked the rope, the workers at the top pulled him up. If he didn't reach the top quickly enough, the force of the **explosion** might kill him.

Central Pacific workers dug a number of tunnels through the Sierra Nevada, but Tunnel No. 6, the Summit Tunnel, was the most challenging. The tunnel was long—more than 1,600 feet long—and the rock was very hard granite. To speed up the process, workers drilled a vertical hole into the mountain in the path of the tunnel and began tunneling outward from the center as well as inward from the ends of the tunnel.

Still, the work was hard and slow. When the heavy snows of winter began to fall, work continued. Many workers lost their lives to avalanches and bitter cold, as well as to the dangerous explosives and the rockfalls they caused. Work continued in spite of the hardships, because time, on this project, was money.

The railroad companies were racing to the finish, because the government was offering them lots of money for every mile of track laid. Each company wanted to lay the longest track possible, so that they could earn the most money. Finally, on May 10, 1869, the railroads met in Promontory Point, Utah. The coast-to-coast railroad was finished at last.

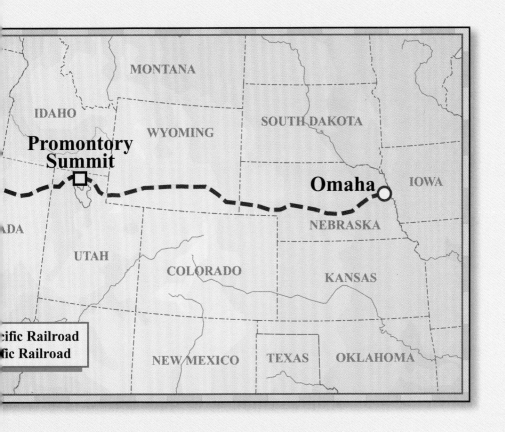

Stop That Train!

During this time, trains continued to run on rails all over the country. Yet they weren't very safe. For one thing, they didn't have good brakes.

To stop a train, a brakeman pulled a lever from inside the train. The lever pushed a block onto the wheels. A brakeman had to be on each train car. The engineer whistled for all the brakemen. Most of the time the brakemen did not pull the lever at the exact same time. This could cause a train to derail.

To stop a train another way, the driver could put the train into reverse, but this action ruined the wheels. An inventor named George Westinghouse found a better way to stop trains. He invented the air brake in 1868.

Diagram of an Air Brake

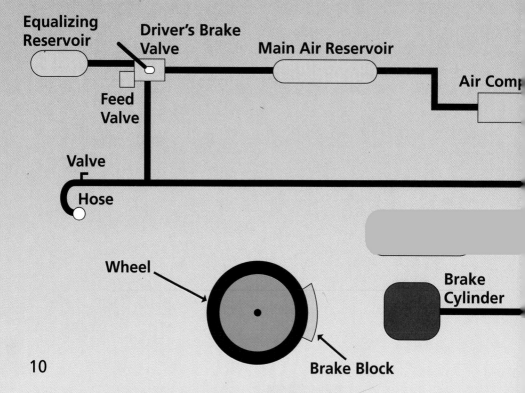

Equalizing Reservoir

Driver's Brake Valve

Main Air Reservoir

Air Comp

Feed Valve

Valve

Hose

Wheel

Brake Cylinder

Brake Block

You might wonder how you can stop a train with air. Here's how. An air compressor is placed in the locomotive, the first car of the train. The compressor is attached to a valve that the engineer controls. When the engineer releases the air, it goes through pipes connected to the rest of the cars on the train. In between each car, the air goes through rubber hoses that can bend with the curves. Inside each car, another valve is sensitive to the flow of air. If the air stops, a brake pad drops onto the wheels of the car. This way, with one touch of a lever, an engineer can engage all the brakes and stop the whole train.

This invention changed trains forever. The U.S. Congress passed a law in 1893 saying that trains had to use air brakes. Today, air brakes are used in trains, buses, streetcars, and even planes in flight.

Air brakes allowed one engineer to control the braking system of an entire train.

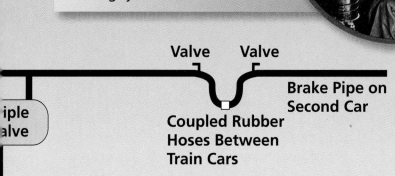

or

Valve   **Valve**

iple
alve

Brake Pipe on Second Car

Coupled Rubber Hoses Between Train Cars

Train Crash!

Even with air brakes, it was still hard to stop a train. This train wreck in Ohio shows just how dangerous it was.

The crash happened on a very cold night in January of 1887. A freight train was heading east when it broke down.

The conductor waited for the train to stop completely. Then he ran forward with a lantern to signal oncoming trains, but he did not get very far. A passenger train traveling more than sixty miles per hour was coming toward him. Even though the engineer of the passenger train pulled the brakes, there was not nearly enough time or space for the

The Baltimore and Ohio Railway Disaster, January 15, 1887, took place near Republic, Ohio.

passenger train to stop. It ran into the freight train, sending the two engines off the tracks. The train cars burst into flames as the hot coals that fueled the engines scattered across the cars. By morning, all of the cars had been burned to a crisp. Hardly any of the passengers survived. Because the freight conductor made a bad decision, the railroads ended up **criticizing** him and he lost his job.

This horrible wreck was not caused by poor brakes. A moving train can take more than a mile to stop. This wreck was caused by bad timing and the lack of useful signals. Railroad safety was improved greatly by the invention of reliable signaling systems.

Train Traffic Jam

To keep trains on schedule in the early days, the railroad companies used a timed system. As one train started out, the next train waited at least ten minutes before leaving, and so on.

This system did not always work. Trains could break down. If the first train broke down, the next would have to try to stop as soon as it saw the broken-down train.

The railroads also decided that the ten-minute wait hurt their business. They could not add more trains unless they made it a shorter wait time. With less time between trains, however, there were more accidents.

Clearly, the railroads needed a better system. Again, George Westinghouse had the answer. He invented the first automatic train signals. This signal system used lights set along the tracks to give directions to the engineer and tell him how fast he could drive. They also tell the engineer if he needs to stop ahead.

Many train wrecks were caused by weak bridges.

Bridge Collapse!

Even if trains were running on schedule and following signals, there were other hazards that could cause wrecks. One such wreck happened because a weak bridge failed in Rhode Island.

In the middle of the night, in April 1873, a large train was rolling toward Providence. It had three cars of freight and five coach cars carrying about one-hundred passengers.

As the train headed for the bridge, disaster struck. Just days before, heavy rains had fallen, **drenching** the area and causing floods. A dam had given way, sending water to erode the supports at the bridge's base.

The rails on top of the bridge had held together. Unfortunately, they had nothing supporting them below. As soon as the train rolled onto the bridge, the bridge collapsed. Most of the train cars fell into the channel. The parts of the train above water burst into flames. Nine people died.

Time Trouble

In the mid-1800s there were no standard time zones. This meant that local towns and counties decided on their own time. They usually went by the sunrise and sunset in the area. Many towns had standard clocks. The standard clock might be a city clock tower. It could also be the time at the general store.

These time differences did not cause any problems—for awhile. People did not travel long distances to work. They did not have telephones to talk with people far away. They did not have radios. But if they were going to catch a train, they needed to know the schedule.

By the 1860s, each railroad company had its own standard time. This meant that the railroad had a set time for each town or state.

Different railroad companies could have different times, which made things hard for a person traveling by train, especially if the traveler had to change trains. The railroads printed a timetable, like the one pictured here. These timetables helped people figure out the time in other cities.

CENTRAL PACIFIC RAILROAD.
NO. 1, TIME CARD NO. 1.
To take effect Monday June 6th, 1864, at 5 A. M.

LELAND STANFORD, President.

1 AM 2 AM 3 A

Wo
Ti
Zo

Time Zones

Train travel and timetables created a new need for a standard time system. The railroads solved this problem in 1883. They created time zones in the United States. This did not mean that people in each town used that time. It meant that the railroads used it. It also meant that people could travel around the country more easily. They could figure out when they would arrive in each city.

The United States adopted official time zones in 1884. That year twenty-seven nations met in Washington, D.C. They created time zones for the entire globe. There are twenty-four time zones. The prime meridian is the first time zone. It runs through Greenwich, England. The first time zone to the east is one hour later than Greenwich. The next time zone to the east is two hours later than Greenwich. The time zones to the west are earlier than Greenwich. You can see this on the map below.

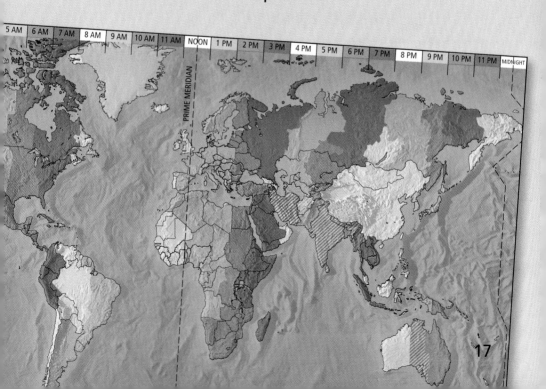

Casey Jones

Train wrecks have always been headline news. On the night of April 30, 1900, Casey Jones was the engineer on a train going from Memphis, Tennessee, to Canton, Mississippi.

When the train pulled out two hours late, Jones wanted to make up for lost time. His fireman, Sim Webb, loaded the engine with coal. Soon, the train **cruised** at 70 miles per hour.

Just then, Jones saw a freight train dead ahead. He yelled for Webb to jump. Jones died in a heroic effort to stop his train. A nearby worker, Wallace Saunders, saw the event and wrote a famous song about Casey Jones.

Trains Today

Today, people ride buses, cars, and planes more than the rails to get to their destination. Trains are still being developed, however, such as one that uses a **hydrogen** fueling system.

Trains will always be an important part of our history—and the stories of the brave people who died building and driving them will continue to inspire us.

Casey Jones is the most famous engineer to die in a train wreck.

The Ballad of Casey Jones

Come all you rounders that want to hear
The story of a brave engineer.
Casey Jones was the rounder's name,
On a six eight wheeler, boys, he won his fame.
The caller called Casey at half past four,
He kissed his wife at the station door,
He mounted to the cabin with the orders in his hand,
And he took his farewell trip to that promised land.

Chorus:
Casey Jones mounted to his cabin
Casey Jones with his orders in his hand
Casey Jones mounted to his cabin,
And he took his farewell trip to the promised land.

So turn on your water and shovel in your coal,
Stick your head out the window, watch those drivers roll;
I'll drive her till she leaves the rail,
For I'm eight hours later by that Western Mail.
When he was within six hours of the place,
There Number Four stared him right in the face.
He turned to his fireman, said Jim, you'd better jump,
For there's two locomotives that are going to bump.

Chorus:
Casey Jones—two locomotives,
Casey Jones—going to bump
Casey Jones—two locomotives,
There're two locomotives that are going to bump.

Glossary

criticizing *v.* finding fault with.

cruised *v.* traveled at the best speed.

drenching *v.* getting something soaking wet.

era *n.* a period of time.

explosion *n.* the process of something bursting open or blowing up.

hydrogen *n.* a colorless, odorless gaseous element that burns easily and weighs less than any other element.